WILD NATURE

DEADLY ANIMALS

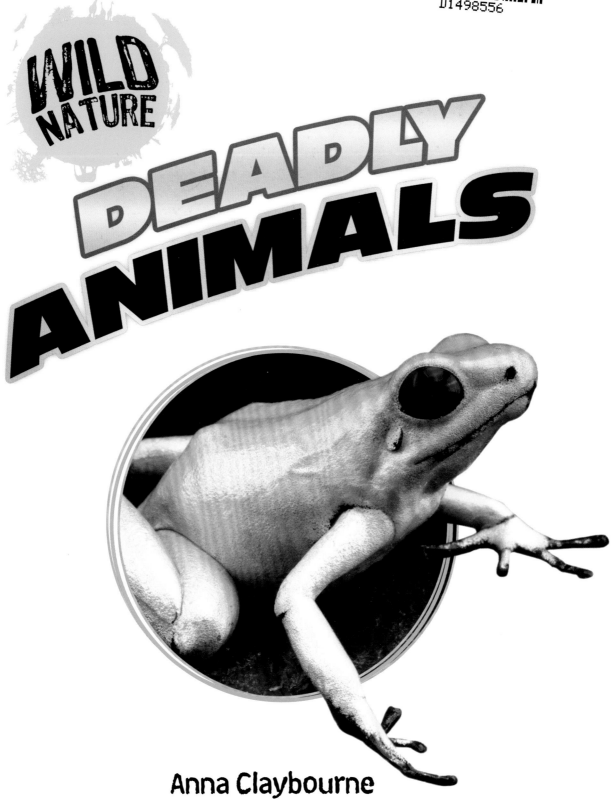

Anna Claybourne

Miles Kelly

First published as *My Top 20 Deadly Animals* in 2011 by Miles Kelly Publishing Ltd
Harding's Barn, Bardfield End Green, Thaxted, Essex, CM6 3PX, UK

This edition published in 2014

10 9 8 7 6 5 4 3 2 1

Publishing Director Belinda Gallagher
Creative Director Jo Cowan
Editorial Director Rosie Neave
Senior Editor Claire Philip
Concept Designer Simon Lee
Volume Designer Kayleigh Allen, Rob Hale
Image Manager Liberty Newton
Production Manager Elizabeth Collins
Reprographics Stephan Davis, Thom Allaway
Assets Lorraine King

ISBN 978-1-78209-500-2

Printed in China

British Library Cataloguing-in-Publication Data
A catalogue record for this book is available from the British Library

ACKNOWLEDGEMENTS
The publishers would like to thank the following sources for the use of their photographs:
Key: (m) = main (i) = inset

Front cover: (main) Image Quest Marine/Alamy, (Wild Nature animal globe) ranker/Shutterstock.com
Back cover: (top) Dennis Donohue/Shutterstock.com, (bottom) Michael Zysman/Shutterstock.com
Page 1 reptiles4all/Shutterstock.com
Pages 4–5 (clockwise from bottom left) Anup Shah/naturepl.com, Piotr Naskrecki/Minden Pictures/FLPA,
Brandon Cole/naturepl.com, Michio Hoshino/Minden Pictures/FLPA, Thomas Marent/Minden Pictures/FLPA
Black rhinoceros (m) Tony Heald/naturepl.com, (i) Michael Hutchinson/naturepl.com
Chimpanzee (m) Anup Shah/naturepl.com, (i) Anup Shah/naturepl.com
Humboldt squid (m) Richard Herrmann/Photolibrary.com, (i) Norbert Wu/Minden Pictures/FLPA
Emerald tree boa (m) Piotr Naskrecki/Minden Pictures/FLPA, (i) Karl Switak/NHPA.com
Mosquito (m) CDC/PHIL/Corbis, (i) David Scharf/Photolibrary.com
Greater false vampire bat (m) Stephen Dalton/naturepl.com
Cassowary (m) Pete Oxford/Minden Pictures/FLPA
Portuguese Man o' War (m) Wolfgang Poelzer/Photolibrary.com, (i) Panda Photo/FLPA
Golden poison dart frog (m) Thomas Marent/Minden Pictures/FLPA, (i) Michael & Patricia Fogden/
Minden Pictures/FLPA
Komodo dragon (m) R.Dirscherl/FLPA, (i) Conrad Maufe/naturepl.com
Safari ant (m) Piotr Naskrecki/Minden Pictures/FLPA, (i) Martin Dohrn/naturepl.com
Blue-ringed octopus (m) Chris Newbert/Minden Pictures/FLPA, (i) WaterFrame/Alamy
Mojave rattlesnake (m) John Cancalosi/Photolibrary.com
Sydney funnel-web spider (m) A.N.T. Photo Library/NHPA.com
Bald eagle (m) Corbis/Photolibrary.com, (i) Jim Brandenburg/Minden Pictures/FLPA
Brown bear (m) AlaskaStock/Photolibrary.com, (i) Eric Baccega/naturepl.com
Geography cone (m) Jeff Rotman/naturepl.com, (i) Visuals Unlimited/naturepl.com
Thick-tailed scorpion (m) Tony Phelps/naturepl.com, (i) Stephen Dalton/naturepl.com
Mountain lion (m) Jurgen & Christine Sohns/FLPA, (i) Jurgen & Christine Sohns/FLPA
Wolverine (m) Lynn M. Stone/naturepl.com

Every effort has been made to acknowledge the source and copyright holder of each picture.
Miles Kelly Publishing apologizes for any unintentional errors or omissions.

Made with paper from a sustainable forest

www.mileskelly.net info@mileskelly.net

CONTENTS

RUN FOR YOUR LIFE: KILLER CREATURES

We don't normally run into deadly animals, but they're out there! The natural world has hundreds of species of killer creatures that you wouldn't want to meet on a dark night – or at any time at all!

Unlike humans, many wild animals have bodies equipped with dangerous weapons, from razor-sharp claws, talons and teeth to powerful poison and venom that can paralyze you in minutes. But don't panic – dangerous wild animals are unlikely to attack you. Most would rather run away and hide from humans. Sadly, deadly animals are often unnecessarily killed because people misunderstand and fear them.

1

TEETH
Big, sharp teeth help many animals catch their prey (the animals they eat). Animals such as tigers, bears and chimpanzees have teeth that can give a deadly bite.

SCARY TEETH

↗ The bald eagle's tearing talons are important hunting tools, used to snatch their unsuspecting fish prey from the water.

↖ Tigers have enormous, terrifying teeth and use them to kill prey such as deer, wild pigs and young buffalo.

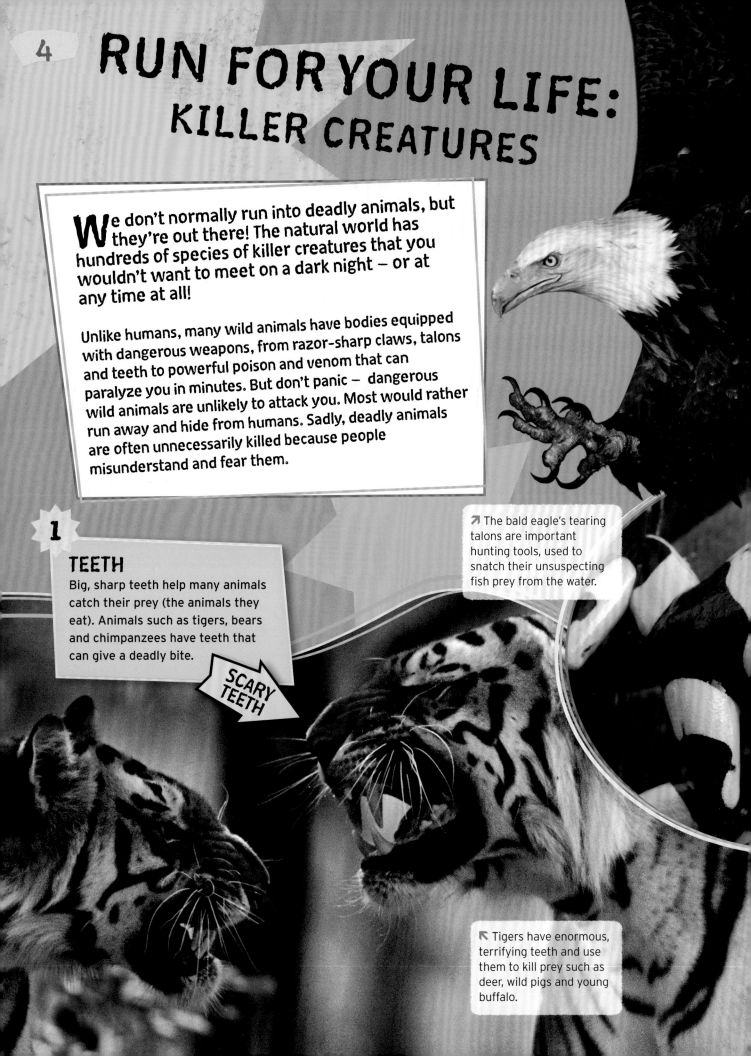

2 VENOM

SHARP BITE

A huge number of animals, such as snakes, spiders and scorpions, have developed deadly venom, which their bodies make in special glands. It's injected into enemies using needle-like fangs, beaks, stings or sharp spines and is often strong enough to kill humans.

→ Venomous snakes such as rattlesnakes inject venom deep into the flesh of their victims using their large fangs.

3 POISON

Unlike venom, poison isn't injected into the victim. It is taken into the body by being eaten, breathed in, or absorbed through skin. Many poisonous animals are brightly coloured and patterned to warn predators of their deadliness.

KILLER MEAL

↓ Long claws help bears tear into the flesh of fish or other prey, and also make good weapons for fighting attackers.

↖ Poison-dart frogs use colours and patterns to warn predators of their toxicity. If their attackers decide to eat them, it may be their last ever meal.

4 CLAWS

FIERCE CLAWS

Many animals such as brown bears have big, sharp claws that help them tear, stab or grab other animals. Even a bird, such as an eagle or cassowary, can have killer claws.

Rhinos are large, lumbering vegetarians that like to munch plants and wallow in mud... what's so deadly about that? Well nothing – as long as you don't get in their way! If a black rhino is annoyed, scared or confused, it will charge – and 1000 kilograms of grumpy rhino thundering towards you at over 50 kilometres per hour is very dangerous indeed.

BRUTE STRENGTH

TAKE THAT...

Rhinos often fight each other to the death to claim territory. These male white rhinos (close cousins of black rhinos) are wrestling with their heads and horns.

SPECIAL FEATURES

SIZE: An adult male black rhino is the size and weight of a car, so if it charges at you and makes contact, you'll be squashed flat!

SPEED: The rhino's top speed of around 50 km/h is much faster than humans can run, making a charging rhino seriously scary.

Black rhinoceros

Scientific name: *Diceros bicornis*
Type: Mammal
Lifespan: 25–40 years in the wild, longer in captivity
Length: 3–3.8 m
Weight: 800–1300 kg
Range: Southern and eastern Africa
Status: Critically endangered

'STAR FACT

One reason rhinos are endangered is because people sometimes kill them to steal their horns. They grind up the horns to make traditional medicines. This is illegal.

CHARGE...

Watch out! Here comes a black rhino charging at top speed. Rhinos run on their tiptoes to help them go as fast as possible.

HORN: Rhinos use their horns to threaten each other, to fight and to defend themselves. When a rhino charges, its horn is the part that hits the target first!

AGGRESSION: Black rhinos are easily angered, and often charge at other animals. As their eyesight is poor some even charge at trees by mistake!

In the wild, gangs of chimpanzees scream, hoot and chase prey through the jungle. These large apes are closely related to humans, and use their great intelligence to organize hunts. Each chimp takes its own role in the hunting team. Chimpanzees are incredibly strong animals, and can be very deadly. In captivity, they have been known to attack humans, biting with their sharp teeth and tearing at their victim with their powerful hands.

CLEVER HUNTER

MUNCH...

Chimpanzees hunt to find prey in the African jungles where they live. This chimp has caught a red colobus monkey to eat.

SPECIAL FEATURES

STRENGTH: Chimpanzees have longer, stronger muscles than humans – they may be up to twice as strong as a human of the same weight.

HANDS: A chimp's large, human-like hands are very strong. They help the chimp dart through the treetops and grab tightly onto its prey.

Chimpanzee

Scientific name: *Pan troglodytes*
Type: Mammal
Lifespan: 40–60 years
Length: Up to 1.2 m
Weight: Up to 70 kg
Range: Central and western Africa
Status: Endangered

'STAR FACT

People used to think chimps were gentle vegetarians, grazing on fruit. Then a scientist called Jane Goodall studied them and discovered that they hunt and eat meat, too.

STAY AWAY...

This male chimp is making a 'screaming' face, showing his teeth. This means he's excited, agitated or scared, and could be dangerous.

TEAMWORK: In the wild, chimps live in groups of up to 80 individuals. They can team up and work together to surround and trap prey animals such as monkeys.

INTELLIGENCE: Chimps are clever animals and are skilled at making and using tools. They can communicate with sounds and facial expressions.

This curious-looking sea monster is a Humboldt squid — a fast, fierce hunter bristling with deadly weapons. It grows up to 4 metres long including its strong, stubby tentacles, and hunts in groups to attack large prey such as other squid or sharks. These squid have been known to attack human divers and fishermen, using their sharp, stabbing beaks to bite them.

SCARY SQUIRTER

SQUIRT...

A Humboldt squid speeds along at up to 24 km/h by squirting a jet of water out of a tube inside its body called a siphon. It can also squirt a dark, inky substance to confuse enemies or prey.

SPECIAL FEATURES

BEAK: Squid have parrot-like beaks with razor-sharp edges between their tentacles, used to slice open and eat prey.

SUCKERS: The tooth-edged suckers all over a Humboldt squid's tentacles help it clamp onto its prey. Fish are held by suction and barb-like teeth.

Humboldt squid

Scientific name: *Dosidicus gigas*
Type: Mollusc
Lifespan: 1–2 years
Length: Up to 4 m, including tentacles
Weight: Up to 45 kg
Range: Eastern Pacific Ocean
Status: Not yet classified

STAR FACT

Like most squid, the Humboldt can change colour. Patterns flash across its skin at lightning speed. Experts think squid use this as a way of signalling to each other.

YIKES...

The squid's tentacles are covered with strong suckers, edged with razor-sharp 'teeth' – around 25,000 of them altogether!

CO-OPERATION: Squid are intelligent invertebrates (animals lacking backbones). Humboldt squid are good at communicating with each other and hunt in teams.

EYESIGHT: The Humboldt squid's huge, beady eyes help it to spot prey in the murky, deep seas where it lives.

Although this large snake has no venom, its sharp teeth can give a painful bite and its strong coils can give a deadly squeeze. It's an emerald tree boa – a member of the boa constrictor family. These snakes wrap themselves around their prey and squeeze hard so the captured animal can't breathe. Once the prey is dead, the snake opens wide and swallows it down. Emerald tree boas are renowned for their colouring – bright emerald green, with white zigzag 'lightning' markings and a bright yellow underside.

GREEN SQUEEZER

WAITING GAME...

An emerald tree boa lies coiled in a tree, waiting for prey animals such as mice, birds and monkeys to pass by.

'STAR FACT

Emerald tree boas spend their entire lives up in the trees, never coming down to the ground. They feed, sleep and have their babies in the branches.

SPECIAL FEATURES

HEAT PITS: Like many snakes, the boa has heat-detecting sensors just above its mouth. They can sense the body heat of animals nearby.

TEETH: The boa uses its large front teeth to grab and hold tightly onto its prey as it wraps its body around and starts squeezing.

Emerald tree boa

Scientific name: *Corallus caninus*
Type: Reptile
Lifespan: 15–20 years
Length: About 2 m
Weight: 1–2 kg
Range: South American rainforests
Status: Least concern

TRAPPED...

This unlucky mouse is being squeezed to death by an emerald tree boa, before being swallowed whole.

STRENGTH: Boas have strong muscles for squeezing their prey. Emerald tree boas don't normally kill people, but larger boas such as the boa constrictor can.

JAW: Boas have jaws that can unhinge from each other and stretch wide open, allowing them to swallow animals bigger than their own heads.

You're looking at the deadliest animal on the planet, a killer of millions of people every year. It's not a growling big cat, a great white shark or a grizzly bear. It's a tiny, buzzing bug – the mosquito. Although maybe we shouldn't blame the mozzie itself, as it's not the true killer. Instead, its bite spreads germs, which cause deadly diseases such as malaria and dengue fever.

GERM SPREADER

HERE I COME...

A close-up view of *Anopheles gambiae*, the most common type of malaria mosquito in Africa, where malaria is a big problem.

SPECIAL FEATURES

PROBOSCIS: The mosquito's long, needle-like proboscis can easily stab into human skin, as well as plant stems or fruits.

EYES: Like other flies, mosquitoes have huge (for their body size) 'compound' eyes made up of lots of many smaller eyes fused together.

Mosquito

Scientific name: *Aedes,*
Anopheles and others
Type: Insect
Lifespan: Up to 3 months
Length: 8 mm
Weight: 0.002 g
Range: Most warm and tropical
parts of the world
Status: Least concern

SLURP...

Mosquitoes spread diseases when they stick their straw-like mouths into our skin to feed on blood, leaving some of their saliva behind.

STAR FACT

Mosquitoes don't actually feed mainly on blood – they suck fruit juices and plant sap. But a female mosquito needs to feed on blood before she can lay eggs. All the mozzies that bite us are females.

GERMS: Not all mosquitoes carry malaria, but those that do have plasmodium, a type of tiny animal, living in their bodies.

WINGS: Mozzies are champion flyers. They can keep airborne for hours, and beat their wings around 500 times per second, making a high whining sound.

Other bats don't hang around in the caves where the greater false vampire bat lives – they're scared of being eaten! Few bats are fierce predators, but this one is. It hunts other small mammals, fish, frogs and birds and catches them by flitting around just above the ground at night, and grabbing prey as it goes by. False vampire bats are one of the few types of bat that actually eat the flesh of their prey.

SUDDEN DEATH

Greater false vampire bat

Scientific name: Megaderma lyra
Type: Mammal
Lifespan: Up to 12 years
Length: Head-body 10 cm, wingspan 30 cm
Weight: 40–50 g
Range: Various parts of Asia
Status: Least concern

CHOMP...

A greater false vampire bat munches on the flesh of a mouse it has caught, its slurping mouth dripping with blood.

'STAR FACT

Don't be fooled by this bat's scary name! There are bats that suck people's blood, but this isn't one of them – though it does have sharp, fang-like teeth.

SPECIAL FEATURES

TEETH: The bat has sharp teeth, which it uses to bite its prey. Some reports say it sucks out the blood first, then eats the body.

ECHOLOCATION: Many bats navigate by making high-pitched sounds and detecting the echoes that bounce back from objects.

BIG BIRD

This is the second biggest bird in the world, after the ostrich, and is on record as being the most dangerous! It's a cassowary – a large flightless bird that runs on its two super-strong legs. Although it looks more comical than deadly, it could give you a serious kick with its killer claw if you get too close to it or its babies.

Cassowary

Scientific name: *Casuarius casuarius*
Type: Bird
Lifespan: About 50 years
Height: About 1.5 m
Weight: About 50 kg
Range: Parts of Southeast Asia and Australia
Status: Vulnerable

'STAR 'FACT

Cassowaries look dumpy, but they're actually amazing athletes. They can run at up to 50 km/h, and jump high in the air, leaping over obstacles as high as themselves.

WATCH OUT...

Never try to feed a cassowary! This will make it expect more food, and it could try to attack you.

SPECIAL FEATURES

CLAW: On the cassowary's large, strong feet are three clawed toes. The middle claw is the main weapon – it's up to 8 cm long and razor-sharp.

CASQUE: This bird has a hard, crest-like part on the top of its head, which it uses to ram into anything that gets in its way.

Deadly animals don't get much weirder than the peculiar-looking **Portuguese Man o' War.** It's often called a jellyfish, but it's actually a siphonophore, a group of tiny creatures living together like a single animal. It is named after a type of old-fashioned sailing ship because of its inflatable, transparent sail. The Man o' War floats along aimlessly on the surface of the sea, with its venomous tentacles dangling below.

STINGING SAILER

'STAR FACT

This strange animal doesn't decide where to go – it has no brain and can't move itself, so it simply travels wherever the waves and wind take it!

STING...

A Portuguese Man o' War's sail bobs on the water, with its jelly-like body parts and stinging tentacles trailing in the water.

SPECIAL FEATURES

SAIL: The inflatable sail is unlike anything found on other animals. It's often purple or blue-tinged, giving this animal the nickname 'bluebottle'.

VENOM: The Portuguese Man o' War's tentacles are covered in stinging cells that deliver venom. The sting is painful and can be deadly to humans.

Portuguese Man o' War

Scientific name: *Physalia physalis*
Type: Siphonophore
Lifespan: Up to 1 year
Length: Sail 10–30 cm,
   tentacles 10–20 m
Weight: Approximately 1 kg
Range: Warm oceans worldwide
Status: Least concern

DEADLY SWARM...

As Portuguese Man o' Wars rely on the wind to move, they often get blown together into huge groups, covering parts of the ocean surface.

LONG TENTACLES: The tentacles can dangle as far as 22 m below the sail. As they drift through the water, fish, shrimps and other prey get caught.

SWARMING: A big group of Portuguese Man o' Wars can make a large area of sea or coastline out of bounds to humans because of the danger of stings.

There is a very good reason that this little golden poison dart frog has the scientific name 'terribilis'. The deadly chemicals in its skin make it one of the world's most poisonous animals. Any animal that grabs the frog in its mouth will feel a painful burning sensation, and may even die a horrible death from heart failure and loss of muscle function (paralysis).

DEADLY POISONER

'STAR FACT

These strange creatures are called 'dart frogs' because local people use the frog's toxins to make poison-tipped darts for hunting. One dart can kill a large monkey or bird in just a few minutes.

BRIGHT...

The golden poison dart frog gets its name from its bright yellow colour. However, not all golden poison dart frogs are yellow! Some are pale green or orange instead.

SPECIAL FEATURES

POISON: The poisons in a golden poison dart frog's skin are called batrachotoxins. One frog has enough of these in its skin to kill ten humans.

COLOUR: Like many poisonous animals, golden poison dart frogs are brightly coloured to warn predators they'll taste terrible.

Golden poison dart frog

Scientific name: *Phyllobates terribilis*
Type: Amphibian
Lifespan: 2–3 years
Length: About 4 cm
Weight: About 20 g
Range: Colombia, in South America
Status: Endangered

GET OFF...

There are several types of brightly coloured, poisonous frogs. These male strawberry poison dart frogs from Costa Rica are fighting over territory.

PUSHING POWER: Male poison dart frogs fight by pushing and shoving! They press their hands into each other's faces and necks as hard as they can.

TONGUE: Poison dart frogs use their sticky tongues to grab their prey, such as ants and other insects. They get their poison from the ants they eat.

This 'dragon' isn't really a dragon — it's the world's biggest lizard, growing up to 3 metres in length. Instead of breathing fire, it dribbles disgusting, germ-filled drool. It's a rare beast, living only on the Indonesian island of Komodo and three other islands. Komodo dragons have a deadly bite and strong claws, and also use their tails to knock down prey. They can kill large animals such as deer, goats and even buffalos, and they sometimes attack people.

DROOLING DRAGON

DELICIOUS...

A Komodo dragon's favourite food is carrion – the bodies of animals that have already died. Sometimes they even dig up human bodies from graveyards!

'STAR FACT

Komodo dragons are gulping gluttons! One dragon can eat up to 80 percent of its own body weight in one go. Then it lies in a warm place to digest its huge meal.

SPECIAL FEATURES

TEETH: The Komodo dragon has about 60 sharp teeth that are brilliant for grabbing and tearing off chunks of meat, which it gulps down whole.

GERMS: There are several types of bacteria in the dragon's saliva and scientists used to think this was the main way Komodos killed their prey.

Komodo dragon

Scientific name: *Varanus komodoensis*
Type: Reptile
Lifespan: 30–40 years
Length: 2–3 m, including tail
Weight: About 70 kg
Range: Indonesia, in Southeast Asia
Status: Vulnerable

SLOBBER...

The dragon's mouth releases a lot of slippery, stinky saliva to help huge lumps of dead animal slide down its throat more easily – yuk!

VENOM: Recently, scientists have discovered that Komodo dragons also have a venomous bite, like some snakes do – though the venom is quite weak.

TONGUE: The Komodo has a yellow, forked tongue that darts in and out of its mouth, used to detect the smell of dead or dying animals over long distances.

You may have heard of killer ants marching in their millions, destroying everything in their path. This isn't a myth — it really happens, and the ants that do this are called safari ants. They are found in Africa and Asia, and build anthills to live in. But when they run out of food, they go on the move. A marching mass of up to 20 million ants swarms through forests, fields, villages and even houses.

ON THE MARCH

SWARM...

As they march, the ants surround and gobble up anything that's in their way. Here they are attacking termites in their nest.

SPECIAL FEATURES

JAWS: Like most ants, safari ants can sting, but they mainly use their powerful jaws for attacking and killing prey.

STRENGTH: Ants are very strong insects. Safari soldier ants' jaws are so strong that people have used them as 'stitches' to hold wounds closed.

'STAR FACT

Marching safari ants can even surround and kill people. They don't move fast enough to chase you, but anyone who can't move fast could get swarmed over and eaten.

Safari ant

Scientific name: *Dorylus* (several species)
Type: Insect
Lifespan: Workers a few months, queens 10-plus years
Length: 6–12 mm
Weight: 3–5 mg
Range: Parts of Africa and Asia
Status: Least concern

KILLER JAWS...

Some of the safari ants are soldiers, with extra-large, meat-munching jaws. The worker ants have quite big jaws too.

SENSE OF SMELL: Safari ants are blind, but they communicate with each other by releasing chemicals and picking up on each other's scents.

TEAMWORK: Ants are social animals that do everything together. This means they can kill animals much bigger than themselves.

When you think of a killer octopus, you might imagine a giant, ship-wrestling sea monster. But the blue-ringed octopus, the deadliest in the world, is tiny. It's just 10–20 centimetres across, and could sit in your hand. But if it gave you a single bite with its venomous beak, you'd be struggling to survive within a few minutes.

ROCK-POOL BITER

DANGER...

The blue-ringed octopus actually only has blue rings when it is annoyed and about to attack. Like other octopuses and squid, it can change its skin colour quickly.

SPECIAL FEATURES

COLOUR CELLS: Chromatophores are special cells in an octopus or squid's skin. They can shrink or enlarge to make different colour patterns.

BEAK: This octopus bites with a very sharp, pointed beak in the middle of its tentacles. Sometimes, the victim doesn't even feel it.

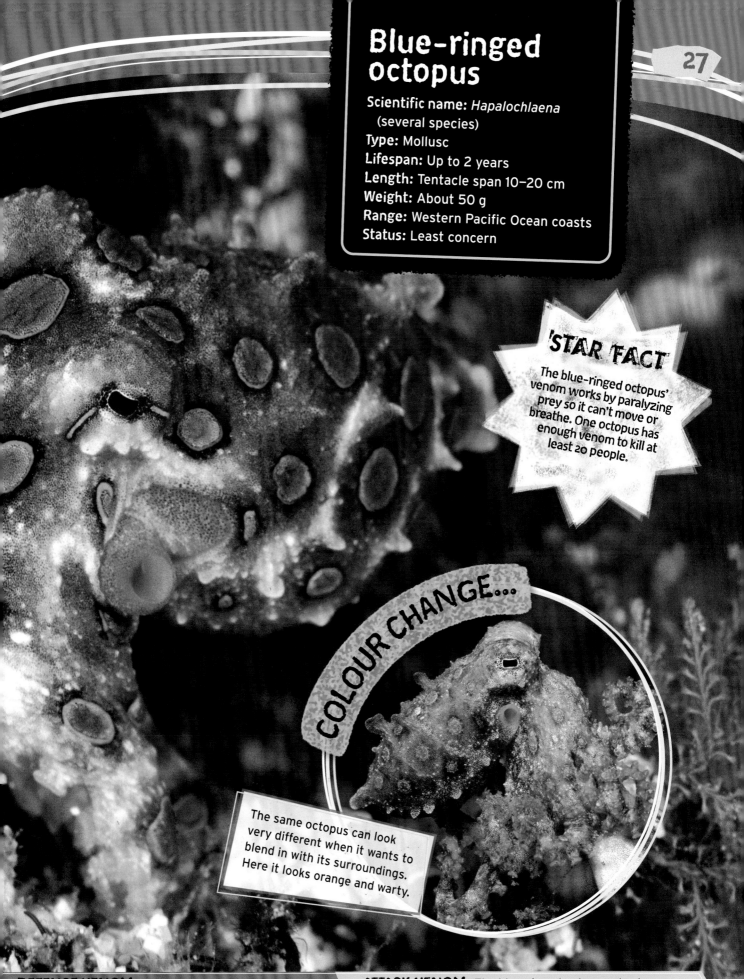

Blue-ringed octopus

Scientific name: *Hapalochlaena* (several species)
Type: Mollusc
Lifespan: Up to 2 years
Length: Tentacle span 10–20 cm
Weight: About 50 g
Range: Western Pacific Ocean coasts
Status: Least concern

'STAR FACT

The blue-ringed octopus' venom works by paralyzing prey so it can't move or breathe. One octopus has enough venom to kill at least 20 people.

COLOUR CHANGE...

The same octopus can look very different when it wants to blend in with its surroundings. Here it looks orange and warty.

DEFENCE VENOM: The killer venom in this octopus' bite is called tetrodotoxin and is used when the animal needs to defend itself against predators.

ATTACK VENOM: The blue-ringed octopus also has a weaker venom for killing the small creatures it eats – crabs, prawns and little fish.

Across the American southwest, people fear the deadly rattlesnake. There are several rattlesnake species, but the Mojave rattlesnake has particularly nasty venom. Rattlesnakes jab their long, sharp fangs deep into their victims' muscles, blood vessels and nerves. They mainly use their deadly bite for killing prey — small lizards and rats — but if you attempt to pick one up, it will bite you!

WARNING RATTLE

Mojave rattlesnake

Scientific name: *Crotalus scutulatus*
Type: Reptile
Lifespan: 20–25 years
Length: Up to 1.3 m
Weight: 4–5 kg
Range: Southwestern USA and parts of Mexico
Status: Least concern

STAR FACT

Rattlesnakes get their name because they have rings of fingernail-like material around the ends of their tails, which they can shake and rattle as a warning.

HISSSSS...

This Mojave rattlesnake is about to attack. It opens its mouth wide, bares its long, venom-injecting fangs, and darts forward.

SPECIAL FEATURES

VENOM: The Mojave rattlesnake's venomous bite makes your muscles feel so weak it can be hard to move or breathe.

RATTLE: A new ring is added to the rattle each time the snake sheds its skin. Young snakes have smaller rattles than older snakes.

FATAL FANGS

If you're terrified of spiders, you might have to cover this page up! This is a Sydney funnel-web, one of the most dangerous spiders in the world, rearing up in an aggressive pose and displaying its deadly fangs. This species only lives in Australia, where people often encounter it. Luckily an antivenom has been developed to treat bites and stop the deadly effects of the funnel-web's toxins.

'STAR FACT

The funnel-web spider gets its name from the tube-shaped web it weaves to live in. The web has long strands of spider silk stretching away from it. The spider can feel if anything brushes against them.

RUN AWAY...

Sydney funnel-web spiders can be extremely aggressive, and will bite if they are picked up or bothered. Around 14 people are known to have died from their bites.

Sydney funnel-web spider

Scientific name: *Atrax robustus*
Type: Arachnid
Lifespan: Males up to 1 year, females 10-plus years
Legspan: Up to 8 cm
Weight: About 10 g
Range: Eastern Australia
Status: Least concern

SPECIAL FEATURES

FANGS: The funnel-web spider has two sharp, hollow fangs, each up to 5 mm long, for injecting venom from venom glands into its victim's skin.

VENOM: The funnel-web's venom is called atraxotoxin – it causes uncontrollable twitching and can be fatal to humans.

For a fish, swimming along near the surface of a sunny lake in North America, a bald eagle attack comes out of nowhere. Suddenly, two huge yellow feet with massive, sharp, black claws crash into the water, clamp around the fish and carry it high into the air. This is how a bald eagle, one of the biggest of all birds of prey, catches its dinner.

TALONED TERROR

OI, GET OFF...

Bald eagles' favourite food is fish, but in winter they often eat carrion, or dead animals. These eagles are fighting over a delicious dead deer.

'STAR FACT

Bald eagles are not actually bald. Their name refers to the white feathers on their heads, and comes from an older meaning of 'bald'.

SPECIAL FEATURES

TALONS: The bald eagle's big, powerful feet have long, sharp, curved claws that allow the bird to grip slippery fish tightly.

BEAK: The strong, hooked beak is sharp and pointed for biting into and tearing at meat – though the eagle mainly uses its feet for hunting.

Bald eagle

Scientific name: *Haliaeetus leucocephalus*

Type: Bird

Lifespan: About 30 years in the wild, up to 45 years in captivity

Length: Body up to 1 m, wingspan up to 2.3 m

Weight: Up to 7 kg

Range: Most of North America

Status: Least concern

YUMMY...

As its super-keen eyes spot a fish, the bald eagle zooms down to just above the water, then spreads its wings and stretches out its talons to land in exactly the right spot.

EYESIGHT: Like all eagles, the bald eagle has brilliant eyesight. Its eyes are about the same size as a human's but it can see several times better than we can.

WINGS: This eagle's mighty wingspan is wider than the height of an adult man! The wings let the bird soar and swoop down on prey at more than 150 km/h.

A 3-metre-tall brown bear standing on its hind legs and roaring is one of the world's scariest animal sights. There are several types of brown bear and some are bigger than others. The biggest, such as the Kodiak bear found in Alaska, are incredibly powerful predators, and sometimes kill humans. Brown bears bare their sharp teeth and roar to defend themselves against predators, such as wolves or mountain lions.

SAVAGE POWER

ROOAARR...

A brown bear's gaping jaws and killer teeth in close-up are a sight you don't want to see in real life!

STAR FACT

Brown bears love honey, as well as fish, berries, fruits, mushrooms, moths, carrion, and larger prey such as goats. They usually only attack humans if they are startled or threatened.

SPECIAL FEATURES

MUSCLES: Even small brown bears are strong, with thick, muscly shoulders and necks. They often win fights with other animals over food.

MOUTH: A brown bear has wide, strong jaws and thick teeth. When attacking, it will often bite and crush its victim's head and face.

Brown bear

Scientific name: *Ursus arctos*
Type: Mammal
Lifespan: 20–25 years in the wild, up to 35 years in captivity
Length: Up to 3 m
Weight: 100–1000 kg
Range: Parts of North America, Asia and Europe
Status: Least concern

BACK OFF...

If they feel their cubs are threatened, female brown bears will become aggressive and fight.

CLAWS: Brown bears have sharp claws up to 15 cm long on their paws. They use them mainly for digging for food but they can also be dangerous weapons.

SENSE OF SMELL: Bears have an amazing sense of smell, even better than that of dogs. They can easily sniff out carrion as well as human food stores.

What is that freaky, alien-like tube sticking out of that seashell? This bizarre-looking beast is a geography cone, a type of sea snail. As well as a squishy, slimy snail body inside its shell, it has a long, tentacle-like part called a proboscis, with a sharp, harpoon-like tooth at the end that can dart out and inject venom into its prey. It may be small, but this sea creature can be deadly to humans, as well as to the unsuspecting animals it hunts.

CONE KILLER

STAR FACT

The geography cone's venom is similar to that of the blue-ringed octopus, and can be lethal to humans. But it also contains some useful chemicals that are being used to make medicines.

DINNER TIME...

Once a geography cone has injected its venom, it sucks its victim up through its tube-like mouth into its stomach. Yum!

SPECIAL FEATURES

PROBOSCIS: The geography cone wanders around, waving its long proboscis towards any creature it thinks might make a nice meal.

TOOTH: This animal's venom is actually injected by a single tooth at the tip of the proboscis that can stick out when needed.

Geography cone

Scientific name: *Conus geographus*
Type: Mollusc
Lifespan: About 10 years
Length: 10–15 cm
Weight: About 50 g
Range: Indian and Pacific oceans
Status: Least concern

SEASHELL...

You may have seen geography cones in the form of the beautiful seashell that's left after the snail dies. The shell is covered in mountainous, map-like patterns, which give it its name.

VENOM: The geography cone has the deadliest venom of any sea snail. Its bites are known to have killed at least 30 people.

MOUTH: The snail can open and extend its tube-shaped mouth onto a wide trumpet shape. It uses it like a net, to surround and suck in prey.

The monster creepy-crawly on this page is as long as your hand, and its sting can be deadly. Nearly all kinds of scorpion have a venomous tail stinger, but this type is one of the deadliest. It's a granulated thick-tailed scorpion, found in southern Africa. To attack, it curls its stinging tail forward over the top of its back, and injects its agonizingly painful venom into its prey.

STING IN THE TAIL

'STAR FACT'

The granulated thick-tailed scorpion is the most dangerous scorpion in South Africa, as it often stings and has powerful venom. It kills several people every year.

GRAB AND STING...

This common yellow scorpion is holding its spider prey still with its pincers as it jabs in a lethal venom.

SPECIAL FEATURES

STING: The thick-tailed scorpion has a large, pointed tail sting, called a telson, which it uses to inject a toxic substance.

VENOM: The deadly venom causes a nasty burning pain, which affects the nervous system, making the victim restless and jumpy.

Thick-tailed scorpion

Scientific name: *Parabuthus granulatus*
Type: Arachnid
Lifespan: About 3 years
Length: About 10 cm
Weight: 10–20 g
Range: Southern Africa
Status: Least concern

LOOK OUT...

This scorpion's stinging tail is raised above its back, in an attacking posture – keep away!

PINCERS: Some scorpions have big pincers to hold their prey while they sting it, but the granulated thick-tailed scorpion's pincers are quite small.

HAIR-LIKE SENSORS: Trichobothria are long hair-like parts on the scorpion's body. They can detect the movements made by prey animals in the air.

Crouched on a rocky ledge, a mountain lion waits out of sight until a deer passes below. Then *pounce!* The cat leaps onto its victim, drags it to the ground and kills it with a bite on the back of the neck. The lion's strong back legs help it leap and climb, and with its powerful jaws and terrifying teeth it can hunt animals as big as deer, sheep, horses and sometimes even humans.

LETHAL LEAPER

TASTY...

This mountain lion is tucking into a deer it has just caught and killed. The meat will keep it going for a couple of weeks.

STAR FACT

Mountain lions (also called cougars, pumas or catamounts) are amazing jumpers. They can leap 5 m straight upward into a tree, or up to 12 m (the length of a bus) along the ground.

SPECIAL FEATURES

JAWS: Strong muscles in the mountain lion's head and neck mean it can bite down incredibly hard, breaking through its prey's bones.

TAIL: This beautiful cat has an extremely long, thick, heavy tail which it uses to balance itself as it runs, climbs and jumps.

Mountain lion

Scientific name: *Puma concolor*
Type: Mammal
Lifespan: Up to 12 years in the wild, 20 years in captivity
Length: 1.5–2.5 m
Weight: 30–90 kg
Range: South and Central America and western North America
Status: Endangered in some areas

PIERCING BITE...

Its big, sharp, tiger-like teeth help to make the mountain lion a top predator.

LEAPING LEGS: A mountain lion's back legs are longer and stronger than its front ones. This allows the cat to make long, springy leaps.

STEALTH: Mountain lions are brilliant at hiding, creeping and sneaking up silently on their prey. They like to pounce from a high-up rock or tree branch.

Don't be fooled by this creature's cute appearance! Although it looks a little like a bear, a racoon or a wolf it is actually a wolverine – a strange animal that's about the size of a dog, but more closely related to weasels. Wolverines are scary creatures because they're incredibly strong and fierce, and will attack anything. They are also known as 'devil bears' or 'demons of the north' because of their aggressive reputations.

FIERCE FIGHTER

Wolverine

Scientific name: *Gulo gulo*
Type: Mammal
Lifespan: 8–10 years in the wild, longer in captivity
Length: About 1 m
Weight: 15–30 kg
Range: Far northern areas around the world
Status: Least concern

'STAR 'FACT

The wolverine's scientific name describes this animal well. The name means 'glutton' (an excessively greedy eater). Wolverines will eat all sorts of things!

SNEAK...

Wolverines often chase other hunters away from their prey, and steal it for themselves.

SPECIAL FEATURES

CLAWS: Along with its teeth, the wolverine uses its sharp claws to attack. They can be partly retracted into its paws, then extended out again.

COURAGE: Wolverines are strong for their size and will take on all kinds of large enemies, including bears, wolves and big cats.